MW00442866

Everything
You Need to
Know About

Family
Court

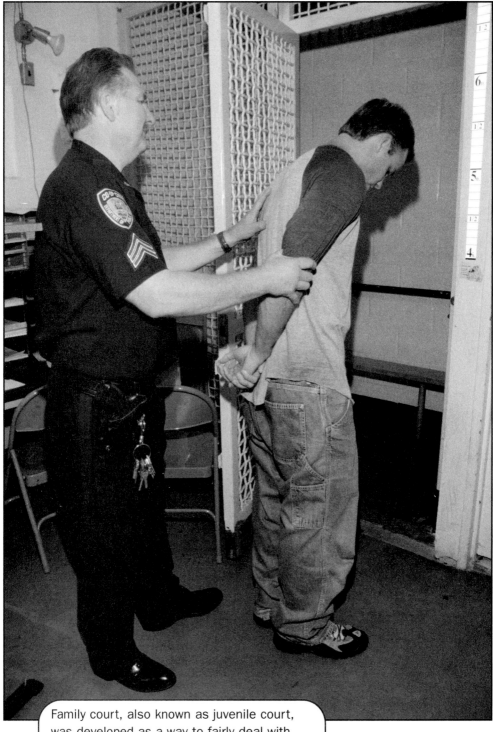

Family court, also known as juvenile court, was developed as a way to fairly deal with youths who have gotten in trouble with the law.

Everything You Need to Know About

Family Court

Anne Bianchi

THE ROSEN PUBLISHING GROUP, INC.
NEW YORK

Published in 2000 by The Rosen Publishing Group, Inc.
29 East 21st Street, New York, NY 10010

Copyright © 2000 by The Rosen Publishing Group, Inc.

First Edition

All rights reserved. No part of this book may be reproduced in any form without permission in writing from the publisher, except by a reviewer.

Library of Congress Cataloging-in-Publication Data

Bianchi, Anne, 1948–
    Everything you need to know about family court / Anne Bianchi.
        p.   cm. — (The need to know library)
    Includes bibliographical references and index.
    Summary: Examines the history and evolution of family court, as well as the continuing debate over the treatment of juveniles in the U.S. leagal system.
    ISBN 0–8239–3163–3
    1. Domestic relations courts — United States — Juvenile literature. [1. Domestic relations courts.] I. Title. II. Series.
KF505.5.Z9 B53 2000
346.7301'5'0269—dc21

                                                                99–039557
                                                                CIP

Manufactured in the United States of America

Contents

	Introduction	6
Chapter One	Not Written in Stone	13
Chapter Two	From Jane Addams to Juvenile Justice	18
Chapter Three	A Noble Experiment?	30
Chapter Four	Changes in Family Court	38
Chapter Five	How Family Court Works	46
	Glossary	58
	For Further Reading	60
	Where to Go for Help	61
	Index	63

Introduction

You've seen the headlines. Everyone has seen the headlines. As this book is being written, in June 1999, there's a new one, this time on the front of *Time* magazine. How to Spot a Troubled Child, the caption practically shouts, in bold lettering over a picture of a forlorn and lonesome-looking teenage boy. Inside the magazine, the article wonders if there is something wrong with the youth of today. Are today's teenagers more violent than ever before, the authors wonder? Are they more troubled? Are they more prone to criminal behavior? Are they more dangerous?

Just three years earlier, all the nation's major weekly news magazines were pondering the same questions. *Newsweek* warned that teens were "running wild in the streets." *U.S. World and News Report* predicted the detonation of a "ticking demographic time bomb." *Time* also spoke of a "teen time bomb" while characterizing teens as "temporary sociopaths—impulsive and immature." Its writers advised Americans to enjoy the current "calm before the storm" before they were "blindsided by [a] bloodbath of teenage violence that is lurking in the future."

The articles reached few definite conclusions. The writers cite some statistics and talk about the events that triggered this debate about teen violence, behavior, and the law. The writers of the earlier article talk about Eric Morse, a five-year-old in Chicago who was dangled from the window of a Chicago housing project and then dropped to his death by two boys, age ten and eleven; and about Robert "Yummy" Sandifer, an eleven-year-old gang member, murderer, and then victim of another juvenile murderer, also in Chicago. The 1999 article discusses in detail the horrifying incidents of mass murder that have taken place at five public schools around the country in recent years. At Littleton, Colorado; at Pearl, Mississippi; at West Paducah, Kentucky; at Springfield, Oregon; and at Jonesboro, Arkansas, young male teens—and in one case, even an eleven-year-old—took guns to their school and opened fire on their schoolmates and teachers, killing and wounding large numbers.

To many people, these acts seemed unthinkable. They reopened an ongoing debate, one that has been conducted for years in homes, classrooms, courts of law, books, the mass media, the halls of state legislatures and even the Capitol in Washington. How should juveniles be treated under the law? (In legal terms, a juvenile is someone who is not yet of legal age, which varies from state to state and depends on the circumstance.) If juveniles commit crimes, should they be treated as adults? Have their cases tried in adult courts? Receive the same sentences that adults would receive, and serve those sentences in the same prisons where adults are incarcerated?

Or should youth, as well as other circumstances, be taken into consideration? Is a thirteen-year-old as responsible for his actions as an adult who behaves the same way? Should he or she be held legally responsible? How about morally? Should this teenager receive the same punishment for his actions as an adult? Does it depend on the crime? Does the teen's youth mean that he or she should be given a second chance when an adult in the same situation might not be? Should the teen be held responsible for his actions, but punished or treated in a different way than an adult would?

What do you think? Difficult questions, aren't they? And even though some people may give their opinions on these matters with absolute confidence and certainty, there really are no easy answers. Every society has debated these questions, and none has come up with any surefire answers yet.

In the United States, this debate has been going on since the birth of the nation. Even before the school shootings, the debate had grown much more intense in recent years. Fueling this intensity is the belief that American society is experiencing an epidemic of criminal violence, much of it committed by young adults or teens—juveniles, in legal terms. Consider, for example, some of the following facts:

- Between 1985 and 1995, the number of juveniles murdered by guns increased by 153 percent.

- In 1998, more than 6,000 students in the United States were expelled from public schools for bringing guns to school.

- In the last two decades, the number of homicides involving juvenile gang violence have increased sevenfold.

- Between 1985 and 1995, the overall homicide rate in the United States increased by almost 20 percent.

- Between 1984 and 1994, the number of juveniles murdered rose by 82 percent.

- African American juveniles constitute approximately one percent of the population of the United States. Yet they constitute 17 percent of homicide victims and more than 30 percent of homicide offenders.

An estimated 75 percent of students report being personally aware of physical attack or bullying (assault) or robbery.

- Between 1989 and 1994, the arrest rate for violent crime—murder, rape, robbery, and aggravated assault—rose more than 46 percent for teenagers. During that same period, the arrest rate for violent crime committed by adults rose just 12 percent. At current rates, the arrest rate for violent crime committed by juveniles will double by the year 2010.

- Since 1987, the risk that a juvenile between the age of 12 and 17 will be the victim of a nonfatal violent crime has risen almost 20 percent.

- An estimated 75 percent of students report being personally aware of physical attack or bullying (assault) or robbery. More than 50 percent say they have witnessed such incidents. Almost 25 percent say that they worry about being the victims of such crimes.

- In a study conducted by the U.S. Centers for Disease Control, one in five students in grades nine through twelve reported carrying a weapon—a gun, knife, or club—to school in the previous month. The reason most commonly given for carrying a weapon to school was "protection."

Since 1995, the rate of violent crime committed by juveniles, particularly the homicide rate, has either leveled off or declined in many areas of the country. Even so, incidents such as the school shootings have reinforced the idea that the United States is a violent and dangerous society, that it is growing ever more violent and dangerous, and that juveniles, especially young men, are the most violent and dangerous members of that society.

So how has society responded? That response can be summarized in two words: Get tough. In 1996, both candidates for the presidency of the United States, Bill Clinton and Bob Dole, proposed that juveniles charged with violent crimes be tried as adults. It was the only response to violent crime that the two candidates agreed on.

Today, all 50 states and the District of Columbia have passed legislation that allows juveniles to be tried and sentenced as adults for certain crimes and under certain circumstances.

These new laws represent a radical change in the way that American society treats juveniles in the legal system. The issue of juvenile crime is controversial because crime cuts to the heart of just about every individual and social relationship that exists in a society—especially family relationships. Consider, for example, just some of the various quick and simple answers that are offered as an explanation for crime—heredity, genetics, race, social environment, poverty, parental and family neglect, inequality of economic and educational opportunity, and the role of the mass media, to name just a few. How one feels about the various explanations for crime influences how one feels about how society should respond to crime, and how one feels criminals should be treated.

The most obvious public place where these issues are played out is in courts of law—specifically, in the criminal courts, where adults who are accused of committing crimes are tried and sentenced. In all the states, juveniles are still, for the most part, handled separately in the legal system. Although the specifics vary from jurisdiction to jurisdiction, the part of the legal system dedicated to juveniles is generally referred to as the juvenile justice system, juvenile court, or family court. How it works (or fails to work), how it got to be the way that it is, and how it is changing to reflect society's concerns are the subject of this book.

Chapter One

Not Written in Stone

Family court has always occupied an unusual place in the American legal system. For much of its history, family court has not really functioned as a true court at all. Instead, many legal historians argue, it has operated more as a social welfare agency than a true court of law. Indeed, that was the specific intention of those who developed the concept of family court. Whether or not this is a good thing depends on your point of view and remains the central issue in the debate over family court and juvenile justice.

Law Evolves

What do you think the goal of the criminal justice system is? What do you think it should be? Specifically, when someone commits a crime, how should he or she be treated? Should he or she be sent to jail? Punished in some other way? Does it depend on the nature of the crime? Does it depend on the circumstances under which the crime is committed? And which of those circumstances should be the most important? Should the race of the person who commits the crime matter? How about if he or she is rich or poor? What if the person is emotionally or mentally ill in ways that makes it difficult or impossible for him to control his behavior or understand the consequences of his actions? What if the person has grown up in conditions of the most terrible abuse, poverty, and neglect? What if the person who commits the criminal act is a child or, as the law refers to her, a juvenile?

These are questions that the American justice system has to answer every day. There is no single answer to any of them. These questions get answered in different ways on different days in different places—in courthouses, police stations, and judge's chambers; in legislative chambers; and in the courts of public opinion, such as television talk shows, news magazines, and the editorial pages of newspapers—across the country.

They have also been answered in different ways at different times in the country's history. Unlike the Ten Commandments, the law in the United States is not written in stone. The law changes as American society changes. It may not always change as quickly as people would like, or change in the exact ways that they would like it to change, but it does change. Evolve might be an even better word, since it often seems that these changes occur slowly, over a long period of time.

Some people have trouble thinking of the law as something that changes or evolves, especially when they think of criminal law. After all, a crime is a wrongful act, right? And what's wrong is always wrong, yesterday, today, and tomorrow, right?

Well, yes, a crime is an act that the law considers wrong. But what exactly the law considers to be wrong can often change considerably over time. What changes equally as much, if not even more, is how the legal system deals with those it believes have committed a crime.

There are many excellent examples of how the law of the United States has changed over time. Some of these concern issues that are still hotly debated, while others concern topics about which it is hard to believe that people—or the law—ever felt differently.

One good example is capital punishment. At some point in their history, most societies have executed individuals for certain kinds of criminal acts. The United States has been no exception. By the second half of the twentieth century, however, most of the world's richest and most powerful nations stopped putting criminals to death, no matter how horrible their crime. The United States joined in this trend between 1966 and 1977. This halt in executions followed a ruling by the U.S. Supreme Court, the nation's highest court, that the death penalty laws of the time in effect violated the Eighth Amendment to the U.S. Constitution. Among other things, the Eighth Amendment guarantees that "cruel and unusual punishments [shall not be] inflicted."

But today, the United States is the only major industrial power in the world that does execute criminals. Since 1977, 38 states have passed new capital punishment laws to meet the Supreme Court's objections to the old laws. Twenty-nine states have carried out executions since then; all told, more than 500 people have been executed in the United States since 1977, 12 of them for crimes committed while they were juveniles. As of late 1999, there were 73 people in the United States on death row awaiting execution for crimes committed while they were juveniles.

You can probably think of other important ways in which the laws of the United States have changed over the course of history. Slavery, for example, was legal until the Thirteenth Amendment to the U.S. Constitution was passed in 1865. Following the Civil War, discrimination on the basis of race remained perfectly legal in most aspects of public life until the civil rights movement of the 1950s and 1960s. Blacks were routinely denied the right to vote until the 1960s. From 1919 to 1933, the manufacture and sale of all alcoholic beverages was illegal in the United States. Women

The United States is the only major industrial power in the world that executes criminals.

were denied the right to vote in the United States until 1920, when the Nineteenth Amendment was passed. Until 1973, women had no right to a legal abortion in the United States. In fact, until the 1960s, birth control was illegal in many states.

What does this have to do with family court? The point is that the law is neither permanent nor perfect. It is an instrument created by human beings and applied by human beings. It makes mistakes, and sometimes it corrects them. Informed, concerned, and involved citizens can act to change it.

Today, as American society debates whether the goal in responding to juvenile crime should be punishment or rehabilitation, major changes are taking place in the way that family court operates.

Chapter Two

From Jane Addams to Juvenile Justice

In 1999, family court celebrated its one-hundredth anniversary in the United States. The first juvenile court in the United States opened in Chicago, Illinois, on July 1, 1899. The court was largely the work of a group of urban reformers associated with Jane Addams, a social worker known for her work with poor people in Chicago. Addams was known best for the establishment of Hull House, a settlement house in Chicago. For her work with poor people in American cities, Addams won the Nobel Peace Prize in 1931.

Settlement houses acted as community, education, health, and recreational centers in poor neighborhoods. Trained social workers, many of whom lived at the settlement house, provided services. Much of their work was directed toward children. Kindergarten, for

For her work with poor people in American cities, Jane Addams won the Nobel Peace Prize in 1931.

example, began in the United States in settlement houses. Health workers established clinics in settlement houses where children could be treated and examined for common childhood illnesses. Settlement houses also provided safe recreational centers, where children could play, and ongoing educational opportunities for adults and older children.

Other People's Children

Addams and reformers like her were responding to tremendous changes in American society. Between 1840 and 1890, the United States experienced what historians refer to as the First Great Wave of Immigration. During that time, millions of immigrants, most of them from northern and western Europe, came to the United States to work and live.

The result was a profound transformation of American society. Large numbers of these immigrants settled in the nation's cities, especially Boston, New York, Chicago, and San Francisco. At the same time, the United States was undergoing a change from a mostly rural, agricultural society to an urban, industrial one.

The result, obviously, was a tremendous rise in the population of America's cities. There was a tremendous increase as well in urban poverty and crime—issues that, to this day, many Americans regard as "big-city problems." Like minority newcomers in any place and time, the immigrants tended to be poor, and they experienced all the usual problems that often accompany poverty, even to this day—violence, substance abuse, damaged family structures, unequal opportunity in education, housing, and employment.

Many Americans had trouble accepting the changes that were taking place in their society. They blamed the problems on immigrants—on the differences in culture, religion, and language that supposedly kept the immigrants from being or becoming "real Americans." Like today, most of the crime was committed by young people, most of them males, which made it easy to blame the nation's rising crime rate on "other people's children"—specifically the children of the new immigrant groups and minority groups. Even Addams—

who described her work as an answer to the question, "how shall we respond to the dreams of youth?"—believed that "four fifths of the children brought into the juvenile court in Chicago are the children of foreigners."

Rehabilitation vs. Punishment

Traditionally, arguments in the United States about the proper role of the criminal justice system center on the goals, or models, of punishment versus rehabilitation. That is, is it the job of the legal and criminal justice system to punish criminals? Or to rehabilitate them by providing them with ways to learn from their mistakes, educate themselves, and become more productive citizens? To a certain extent, these two models have always been at odds.

Supporters of the punishment model focus on the individual's responsibility for his or her own actions, the need to protect society against crime and criminals, and society's obligation to punish those who break its rules. According to the punishment model, those who break the law deserve to be punished for their actions, with much less emphasis on whatever circumstances might have led to the criminal behavior.

Each member of society has a right to be safe from crime, the argument goes, and the best way to do this is to punish those who commit crimes. Believers in the punishment model argue that rehabilitation does not work, that it in fact leads to more crime. They argue that punishment is, in itself, the best kind of rehabilitation. Fear of punishment, they say, keeps individuals from committing crimes in the first place; incarceration (jail time) keeps them off the streets so they cannot commit crimes, while severe punishment deters criminals from committing similar acts again. Punishment, in the form of long prison sentences and even the death penalty, is therefore the best way both to protect society and serve the individual who commits crimes.

Believers in the rehabilitation model disagree. Generally speaking, they tend to focus much more closely on the social causes of crime, specifically on issues such as poverty, childhood abuse, and damaged families. Accordingly, believers in the rehabilitation model focus on ways that the legal system can work to address such issues in the lives of individuals who commit crime. Although they do not dismiss the necessity of jail terms as a punishment for crime, believers in the rehabilitation model do not regard prison as always being the best or most effective way to treat criminals. They would not agree, for example, that longer and harsher prison sentences are necessarily an effective way to deter crime. Instead, they would be much more likely to agree with the idea that social injustices are the leading cause of crime, and that the best way to reduce crime is to address the social problems that lead to it.

With regard to the individuals who commit crimes,

the rehabilitation model is more likely to focus on programs and services intended to help the individual.

Rehabilitation and Juveniles

At various times in history, the criminal justice system
has leaned more toward the rehabilitation model. At other
times, it has leaned more toward the punishment model.
At any one time, elements of both models come into play
in the system. In recent years, the focus has been on
stricter punishment. Examples of this trend include:

- The renewed and more frequent use of capital punishment

- So-called mandatory minimum sentences
  that remove judges' discretion in sentencing
  convicted criminals

- "Three strikes and you're out" laws that
  remove rehabilitation options for repeat
  offenders in favor of long, mandatory sentences

- An overall greater focus on longer prison
  terms as the best response to crime

- The return to long-abandoned methods of
  punishment, such as chain gangs and high-
  way work details

Indeed, since 1980, the number of people in prison in

Constant fighting or domestic violence at home increases the likelihood that children will be involved in violent crime themselves.

the United States has risen from approximately half a million to nearly two million. During that period, the rate of people incarcerated for crimes has risen faster than the rate of crime itself, including violent crime. By the late 1990s, prison construction had become one of the fastest-growing industries in the United States.

Until recently, rehabilitation has been the primary focus of family court and the juvenile justice system. Before Jane Addams established the first juvenile court, children who committed crimes were, for the most part, treated as adults. In general, in the legal system and elsewhere, children were regarded as being essentially small adults.

Addams and her fellow reformers, who were referred to generally as Progressives, set out to change this. In their view, children needed to be treated differently. For many reformers, the rise of crime and poverty in the cities proved that American society needed to change the way it treated children. Reformers proposed, for example, an end to the use of children as labor and worked for legislation to end the practice. They also sought to establish a comprehensive public school system that would guarantee all children access to education.

In trying to understand the causes of crime, the Progressives focused on the role of the social environment, in particular, poverty and family structure. They argued that the social environment could influence children toward crime. Children, it was argued, were much more easily influenced by their social environment than were adults and, in any event, their youth made them less responsible than adults for their actions. They pointed out that since children were not regarded as sufficiently mature to enjoy full civil rights under the Constitution—they could not vote, for example—they should not be held as responsible for their actions, including criminal behavior.

Wise parents, they argued, generally did not require their children to be as responsible as adults in every case, so why should society? If a poor, crime-ridden, or abusive environment played such a large role in causing crime, couldn't children benefit from a different environment? If parents, for whatever reason, proved unable to raise their children well, shouldn't society take on that responsibility? Because of their youth, didn't children who committed crimes deserve as many chances as possible to become rehabilitated? Shouldn't they be given every chance to succeed, especially if their environment had limited their chances from the beginning?

Such thinking led to family court being created as a social welfare agency as much as a criminal court. The first family court in Chicago, which was soon followed by others around the country, was based on the idea that rehabilitation was the most worthwhile goal of treatment for youths who committed crimes. (Such youths are known in legal terms as delinquents.) By 1925, every state but two had established separate courts and procedures for youths who broke the law.

Parens Patriae

Juvenile or family court acted under a legal doctrine known as *parens patriae*. This Latin term is best understood as meaning "the state is the parent" or "the state is the ultimate parent of every child." In this instance, the word "state" should be understood to mean society as a whole, as represented by the government. According to the doctrine of *parens patriae*, the state had the right and duty to intervene in a child's interest if the child's well-being was endangered at home or elsewhere. In such cases, the state would be acting in the best interests of the child and as "the common guardian of the community," as the Pennsylvania Supreme Court put it in the late nineteenth century.

This concept represented a considerable change in the way the law looked at children. Under the law before *parens patriae*, children were little more than the property of their parents. *Parens patriae* marked the beginning of the recognition that children had some legal rights.

One of the ideas behind family court was the assumption that since juvenile crime was, in at least some ways, a failure of parenting or the result of a bad environment, the state would take over the role of parent—a "wise and just parent" was the phrase used by the court's defenders. Relying on the work, guidance, and expertise of trained professionals—judges, social workers, probation officers, psychiatrists, psychologists, physicians, teachers, educators, and other experts in child care and juvenile education—the court would work to create a safe environment for delinquents in which they could be rehabilitated. In many ways, the court took on the role of the family. It is in this sense, also, that juvenile court is often referred to as family court.

Juvenile court acted as a family court in other important ways as well. The area of a court's legal authority is known as its jurisdiction . The jurisdiction of family or juvenile court was not limited to delinquents. Almost immediately, it became obvious that there were many youths who had not necessarily committed crimes but

Relying on the work, guidance, and expertise of trained professionals, the court works to create a safe environment for delinquents.

were nonetheless in need of the intervention of a "wise and just parent." Such juveniles included runaways, orphans, victims of severe abuse or neglect, and the enormous numbers of children who either did not have a safe home where their needs were taken care of or had no home at all.

The result was that over time family courts took on two general kinds of jurisdiction over juveniles: delinquency (juveniles who committed crimes) and dependency (juveniles who had no home or needed to be removed from their homes for their own protection, health, and safety).

In some jurisdictions today, there are divisions of the legal system known specifically as family courts. These courts handle those juveniles who would fall under the dependency portion of a juvenile courts' jurisdiction. In some places, the term family court applies specifically to courts that handle divorces and the child custody issues that arise from them. Some people refer to all the courts that deal with children as child welfare courts. Family court is still used generally to refer to those courts designed specifically to handle the legal problems of juveniles.

Generally speaking, those problems fall under the headings of either delinquency or dependency, and in practice there is considerable overlap between these two areas. Some people distinguish between these two parts of family court by saying that dependency court handles victims, while delinquency court handles victimizers.

However, many veterans of child welfare courts regard dependency court as a sort of gateway to delinquency court. As William Ayers, an educator who has written extensively about juvenile court, puts it, the distinction between dependency and delinquency is often "small, tactical, and technical. Actually there is a powerful connection apparent between a child being a victim one day and becoming a victimizer the next." In the opinion of many who have studied juvenile justice issues, there is no greater risk factor for getting into trouble with the law than having the kind of home life that requires the intervention of a dependency court.

Chapter Three

A Noble Experiment?

As a result of these factors, family court developed a legal process that differed greatly from the way criminal court operated. Some of the differences are demonstrated most clearly in the language that is used in family courts. For example, a juvenile accused of delinquency in family court did not undergo a trial, but a hearing. The hearing was conducted by a judge, and there was no jury. In criminal court, a jury must find the accused "guilty beyond a reasonable doubt." For many years, no such standard applied in family court. A trial in criminal court is a public proceeding, open to outsiders and reported on in the press. A hearing in family court, by contrast, was closed to the public, and its conclusions were confidential. Depending on the jurisdiction, juveniles accused of delinquency offenses did not enjoy all the same legal rights—right to an attorney, protection against self-incrimination and unlawful interrogation, protection against unlawful searches and seizures, the right to confront and cross-examine witnesses—as did an adult accused of a crime.

These differences are reflected even in the way cases in the different kinds of courts are titled. A criminal trial of an adult in the state of New York, for example, would be officially known as The State of New York against John Doe. A trial in criminal court is an adversarial proceeding, meaning that the state is acting against an individual, with the possible consequence that the individual will be deprived of his or her freedom. A delinquency hearing, however, would be officially known as In the Matter of John Doe or In the Interest of John Doe or something similar. The difference in language between the two kinds of cases is important, as it reflects family court's original emphasis on rehabilitation rather than punishment.

But in child welfare courts the state was supposed to be acting in the best interests of the child, even if that child was accused of a crime. A delinquency hearing was not—and still is not—a criminal trial. The idea was that the state was acting for the juvenile, not against him or her. That is why, particularly in the early years of the court, very little emphasis was placed on the juvenile's legal rights. After all, why would juveniles need rights to protect themselves against a "wise and just parent" that was acting in their own interest? Likewise, proceedings in family court were kept confidential to protect the juvenile from whatever "stigma" might be attached to coming under the jurisdiction of a child welfare court.

Similarly, in delinquency hearings, the state did not file charges against the juvenile. Instead, it filed a petition asking the court to take an interest in or come to the aid of the child. Whatever criminal offenses the juvenile had supposedly committed were cited as the reasons why the court needed to intervene. Whereas in criminal court, charges have to be filed by an attorney representing the state, under law almost anyone could file a petition in a child welfare court. For instance, parents might file a petition with the court, alleging that their child is uncontrollable and asking the court to take over the responsibility for raising them. In a delinquency hearing, the judge did not find the juvenile guilty or innocent but determined whether the petition of delinquency was granted. If it was, the youth became a ward of the court, with the court, in the person of the judge, now having the legal authority to determine how he or she would be handled.

In general, hearings in family courts were conducted much more informally than trials in criminal court. Lawyers sometimes took part in such hearings, but less as adversaries than as colleagues. (Jane Addams had hoped that lawyers would not be present in family court at all.) A district attorney might represent the state in presenting evidence of the juvenile's wrongdoing. That same district attorney might also act as the child's probation officer. Frequently, the juvenile received no legal representation at all.

Hearings in family court generally focused as heavily on the advice of trained professionals as it did on evidence of a juvenile's guilt or innocence. Such professionals included probation officers, social workers, psychologists, and others. Based on background research and interviews with the youth in question, family members, and other adults involved in the juvenile's life, they would make an evaluation, or recommendation, of what should be done with the youth. It would then be left to the judge to make a formal decision. These parts of the process are known as the adjudication and disposition.

Until recently, prison terms were not an option for disposition. If the judge thought the case was brought in error or that the child did not need any kind of help, he could dismiss the petition altogether. If the judge granted the petition, he or she then had several options to choose from. The delinquent could be held by the state and placed in special juvenile homes or juvenile halls. State-run vocational schools were also an option. These were residential facilities where the child, it was hoped, could receive education, discipline, vocational training, and counseling. They varied in the degree of freedom they allowed their charges.

Social workers may remove children from their home and place them in a different environment—with other relatives or with foster parents, for example.

The delinquent might be returned to the custody of his parents, with specific measures dictated for treatment and follow-up. For example, the youth might be ordered to undergo psychological counseling, attend school regularly, maintain a curfew at home, and report on a regular schedule to a probation officer. Always, of course, the ideal was rehabilitation rather than punishment. In dependency court, social workers had enormous authority to remove children from their home and place them in a different environment—with other relatives, with foster parents, in group homes, shelters, and large residential institutions, or even to put them up for adoption.

In delinquency matters, judges had enormous freedom in the disposition of cases. Unlike criminal court, there was very little written law telling judges what dispositions they were required to give under specific circumstances. Judges were left with enormous discretion. When delinquents came of legal age, they were no longer under the jurisdiction of a child welfare court. If they broke the law again, they were tried as adults. When juveniles who came under the jurisdiction of dependency court came of age, they were on their own.

In the Matter of Gault

Until the 1960s, most people regarded rehabilitation as a noble ideal, but there was always much disagreement over how well it worked. Critics attacked the workings of the juvenile justice system from both sides. Some argued that the juvenile justice system was too lenient, that it functioned as a "revolving door" in which juveniles who committed crimes came and went again and again through the system without ever being rehabilitated or punished for their crimes. Others argued that insufficient resources were given to the professionals and agencies who worked with the system, so that the goal of rehabilitation could never be met. Still others maintained that the system gave judges too much power and discretion and did not adequately protect the legal rights of juveniles. Overall, a majority of Americans seemed to feel that although the juvenile justice system tried to be a benevolent parent, it was rarely a wise and just one. More often, many people thought, it was neglectful and sometimes even abusive.

These criticisms came to a head in 1967 when the U.S. Supreme Court rendered its opinion in the case of *In re Gault.* (*In re* is a Latin term used in law to mean "in the matter of.") The case had begun in rural Gila County, Arizona, in June 1964. At that time, Gerald Gault was fifteen years old. Bored one afternoon, Gault and a friend decided to make a prank telephone call to a neighbor. The Supreme Court later characterized the call as being of the "irritatingly offensive, adolescent, sex variety."

The local sheriff picked up Gault that same afternoon. He spent the night in jail, without anyone notifying his parents. The next day, he was made to appear at a delinquency hearing, where a probation officer filed a delinquency petition "on his behalf."

In the hearing that followed, the probation officer was also the prosecutor. Gault was never told he had the right to an attorney, so no one trained in the law was present to represent him. He was not told that he had the right to remain silent, and in fact the judge forced him to testify, wherein he allegedly incriminated himself. No member of the public was present to witness the proceedings. No witnesses appeared to testify against Gault. No sworn testimony was given against him. No transcript was made of the proceedings. (A transcript is a formal written record of the court's proceedings; it is often used, for example, to appeal the

The United States Supreme Court is responsible for preserving the intentions of the Constitution and the civil rights of citizens, including juveniles.

decision of a court to a higher court. Gault's parents were told that no transcript was necessary because as a juvenile their son had no right to an appeal.)

After the hearing, Gault was returned to his jail cell. The judge did not reach a decision for several days. At that point, he found Gault delinquent and sentenced him to spend the time until he turned twenty-one—approximately six years—at the state industrial school.

Chapter Four

Changes in Family Court

Had Gerald Gault been an adult, the maximum sentence he could have received for his crime was a $50 fine and/or two months in jail. And that sentence could only have been applied after a trial in which a twelve-member jury, not a judge, found Gault guilty, which could not have happened unless witnesses presented sworn testimony. Gault would have had the right to have an attorney represent him, both in court during the trial, at all the preliminary stages, and even when he was being questioned by police. If Gault wanted an attorney but could not afford one, one would be appointed to represent him. That attorney could have cross-examined witnesses on Gault's behalf. Prior to the trial, Gault could have refused to answer the police's questions unless his attorney was there. A judge or anyone else could not have forced him to testify at trial. And it would have been the responsibility of the police, at the time of Gault's arrest, to advise him of these rights, all of which are guaranteed to U.S. citizens under the Constitution—but not, before In re Gault, to juveniles.

But contrary to what Gault's parents were told, he did have a right to an appeal. (An appeal is a request to have a higher court review the decision of a lower court.) In 1967, Gault's appeal reached the U.S. Supreme Court.

The Supreme Court was scathing in its denunciation of the way Gerald Gault had been treated. "Under our Constitution," the Court said in its decision, "the condition of being a boy does not justify a kangaroo court." And for too many juveniles in too many places, family court had become a kangaroo court, the Supreme Court said.

The result was a complete overhaul of the way family court treats youths in a delinquency proceeding. The Court ruled that in such cases the good intentions of the state were not sufficient to protect a child's interests. In such cases, family court operated as much as a criminal court as it did a social welfare agency. As such, the Supreme Court said, youths in delinquency proceedings were entitled to most of the same constitutional rights as adults who were charged with a crime:

- ◆ They cannot be held in custody without being able to notify their parents or guardian. Written notice of hearings and other proceedings have to be given in a timely fashion.

- ◆ They must be given time to prepare a defense against a delinquency petition.

- They have to be advised of their rights, most importantly, their right to an attorney and their right against self-incrimination. If they want an attorney and cannot afford one, the court must appoint one to represent them without charge.

- They have the right to confront and cross-examine witnesses at delinquency hearings.

A later case, In re Winship, further expanded the constitutional rights of juveniles. During In re Winship, the Supreme Court ruled that the standard used to determine delinquency in a juvenile proceeding had to be the same as what is used to determine guilt in a criminal court—"beyond a reasonable doubt." Before Winship, most judges had used the standard of civil court—a "preponderance of evidence."

The Gault and Winship decisions set the standards by which the delinquency part of family court is run today. It is understood that family court has several goals—punishment of criminals, protection of the community, and rehabilitation.

Accordingly, there is a much greater recognition that family court can be a kind of criminal proceeding and that the youths who are adjudicated there are entitled to constitutional protections. In general, those protections are the same as those received by adults tried in criminal courts, with two important exceptions:

When charged with a crime, juveniles must be informed of their civil rights, most important, their right to an attorney.

- Juveniles do not have an automatic constitutional right to a trial by jury, which for adults is guaranteed by the Sixth Amendment to the Constitution. In most courts, delinquency hearings are conducted only by judges. In some jurisdictions the judge can, however, grant a juvenile's petition to have a jury hear the case.

- Juveniles do not have an automatic constitutional protection against excessive bail, which for adults is guaranteed by the Eighth Amendment. Bail is a bond or payment made to secure the release of someone accused of a crime for the period before the trial. The idea is that since the accused is legally innocent until proven guilty, he or she cannot be held in custody after arrest except under extreme circumstances. Instead, a judge sets bail—determines an amount the accused must pay to secure his or her release until trial. The bail payment is supposed to ensure that the accused shows up for trial. However, juveniles have no right to bail. If a judge determines that the charges are serious enough, he or she can order a juvenile held in protective custody (jail, essentially) until trial.

In general, delinquency proceedings take place with the understanding that the difference between juvenile and criminal courts is "their greater emphasis on rehabilitation, not their exclusive preoccupation with it," as the President's Commission on Law Enforcement and Administration of Justice put it in 1967. More recently, as crime rates have climbed, society has placed an even greater emphasis on punishment and protection at the expense of rehabilitation. One result has been laws allowing juveniles to be tried as adults in certain circumstances.

Changes in Dependency Court

Dependency court has also been overhauled in recent decades. The cause has been greater social recognition of the prevalence of child abuse, combined with the recognition that family court did not work very effectively to help children in such unfortunate circumstances.

For decades after the beginnings of family court in 1899, the power and responsibility for the welfare of abused and neglected children rested in the hands of individual social workers and governmental organizations, often known as child welfare departments, family service organizations, and so on. The social workers and organizations worked with the court, but in most cases the authority for determining how to handle a dependent child rested with them. The most common response was to remove the child from the home and place him in some kind of public institution or foster home.

As with delinquency proceedings, the state took a *parens patriae* role and saw itself as acting in the best interests of the child, but few people thought the system worked well. Abuses were commonplace, institutions were overcrowded and ineffective, juveniles bounced from foster family to foster family, and poor people and minorities believed, with good reason in many cases, that the state was too quick to remove "other people's children" from their homes. A better response, many people argued, would have been programs that addressed the problems assaulting such families— poverty, unemployment, alcohol and substance abuse—while enabling them to stay together.

The result was the Adoption Assistance and Child Welfare Act of 1980, which gives judges explicit authority in dependency court. As in delinquency

In dependency court, judges may rely heavily on the assessments made by experts such as social workers and psychologists.

court, judges may rely heavily on the advice of experts such as social workers and psychologists. Many of these experts work with government agencies—children's welfare and family services, for example—associated with the court.

In making dispositions in dependency court, judges are now required to follow three explicit policies in determining the best interests of the child. They are:

- Family preservation, which means that the first priority of the court and child welfare agencies must be to keep the family together. This may include providing the family with whatever services it might benefit from, such as financial assistance and counseling.

- Family reunification, which means that if the child must be removed from the home, an effort must be made to place him or her with another relative before placement in a foster home or children's shelter. Then, a long-term plan must be made for establishing conditions under which the child can be safely returned home. If, for example, parents are using drugs in the home, they might be made to complete a drug program, undergo testing, and otherwise demonstrate that they can care for their child before the child is returned.

- Preservation planning, which means placing an emphasis on finding a permanent solution to the child's problems. The idea is to establish a stable home for the child and ensure that he or she does not bounce around from foster homes to shelters to home again and again. To do so, a time limit is placed on family reunification services. If a child has been taken from a home and his or her parents cannot comply with the family reunification plan within a specific amount of time, a new, permanent solution must be found. In such cases, the child must be placed in "the most family-like and stable setting available, with adoption being the placement of first choice."

Chapter Five

How Family Court Works

The exact procedures of family court differ from jurisdiction to jurisdiction, but there are basic steps in the process that are the same everywhere.

Intake

The procedure begins with intake. Basically, intake is a general term for the way juveniles are introduced into the court system. For delinquency court, the police are the most common means of referral. Typically, in a given year, somewhere between 80 and 90 percent of the cases in delinquency court will be referred by the police after they have made an arrest.

Depending on the kind of crime committed, the police have a number of choices after arresting a juvenile. About one-third of juveniles arrested are released without ever being referred to court, a process known as station adjustment. The police might, for example, let the juvenile go with a warning. They might talk to his or her parents. They might take steps to get the juvenile into a program that could help him or her.

The youths most likely to receive a station adjustment at this early stage in the process are a class of juveniles referred to as status offenders. A status offender is a juvenile who has committed an act that is considered a crime only because of his or her age. Examples of status offenses include running away from home, drinking alcoholic beverages, violating curfews, sexual promiscuity, or persistent truancy (failure to attend school).

In addition to the police, parents, the victims of crimes, teachers and school officials, probation officers, and social service agencies can also refer juveniles to delinquency court.

Intake Officers

Once a juvenile is referred to the court for delinquency purposes, the decision on how to proceed is made by a probation officer or by a local prosecutor. These individuals are referred to generally as intake officers.

At this point, intake officers investigate what is known about the case and decide if there is enough evidence to proceed. If there isn't, the case is dismissed. If

A status offender is a juvenile who has committed an act that is considered a crime only because of his or her age, such as drinking alcoholic beverages.

there is, the intake officer may decide to ask the court to get involved by declaring the juvenile to be a delinquent.

However, the officer may also decide to process the case informally. Most commonly, the intake officer establishes certain conditions that the juvenile will comply with for a certain amount of time. These might include counseling, enrollment in a drug program, abiding by a curfew, and making satisfactory progress in school. The juvenile's success in meeting these conditions is monitored by a probation officer. If the juvenile meets the conditions, the charges against him or her are dropped. If he or she does not, then the probation officer will most likely bring a formal petition in court.

For dependency court, intake most often begins with a phone call or message by a concerned adult to the local child welfare or social services agency. A social worker then investigates the situation and can file a petition in juvenile or family court if he or she determines that a child is being neglected or abused. Police are also often the source of dependency referrals, as are teachers, school officials, and probation officers.

Detention

While a detention case is in motion, the juvenile can be held in a secure detention facility at the discretion of either the judge or an intake officer. Federal law mandates that this facility be used specifically to hold other juve-

49

niles. Juveniles can be held in adult jails and lock-ups only under certain circumstances, either while awaiting the notification of their parents or awaiting transportation to a juvenile facility. In such cases, the juvenile is supposed to be held for not more than six hours in an area that is not within sight or sound of adult inmates.

If a decision is made to hold a juvenile, he or she must receive a detention hearing within a specific amount of time. In most jurisdictions, that period is twenty-four hours. At the detention hearing, a judge hears the case and determines if it is in the best interest of the community or juvenile that the child continue to be held. As mentioned earlier, juveniles have no automatic right to bail. Approximately 20 percent of juveniles who are formally processed are held in detention prior to the delinquency hearing.

Transfer and Waiver

Every state today has laws that allow juveniles to be tried as adults in criminal court for certain offenses. In some states, the combination of a certain kind of serious crime (usually involving physical violence) and the age of the defendant requires that the case originate in criminal court.

In other circumstances, it is up to the prosecutor or intake officer to decide whether the case should be transferred to criminal court. If the prosecutor determines that it should be, he or she files what is known as a waiver petition. The judge then reviews what is known about the case and decides whether to waive the juvenile court's jurisdiction and allow it to be transferred to criminal court. In general, the most important factors in such decisions are the severity of the crime alleged and the juvenile's history within the criminal justice system. Persistent or repeat offenders are more likely to have their case transferred to criminal court. Nearly one-third of cases referred for delinquency are waived to criminal court. This represents an increase of more than 30 percent since the 1980s.

Adjudication

To adjudicate means simply to decide or settle a matter as a judge. The adjudication of a delinquency proceeding is the judge's decision, or judgement. The judge does not find the youth guilty or not guilty, but delinquent or not. Since the Supreme Court's decision in In re Winship in 1970, the standard of proof for the judge is supposed to be evidence "beyond a reasonable doubt," which is the same standard juries use to determine guilt or innocence in a criminal trial. In some jurisdictions, a juvenile may petition to have his or her case heard by a jury.

According to the most recent statistics compiled by the U.S. Department of Justice, juveniles were adjudicated delinquent in 57 percent of cases in which they were charged with criminal offenses. Status offenders were judged delinquent at only a slightly lower rate.

However, status offenders are much more likely to be diverted out of the system before adjudication. All told, status offenders make up less than 10 percent of the cases referred for adjudication. This is in keeping with the various versions of the Juvenile Justice and Delinquency Prevention Act (JJDPA), which was first passed in 1974 and has been amended several times since then.

One of the goals of the act is the reclassification or diversion of status offenders out of the criminal justice system. This reflects a belief that as the rates of violent crime rose, it no longer made sense to treat status offenders in the exact same way as youths whose actions would be considered criminal if they were adults. The JJDPA also discourages status offenders from being held in secure detention at any time, either while a case is in progress or after adjudication. The only exception is status offenders who have previously violated a court order.

Disposition

Once a juvenile has been judged delinquent, the judge has to decide what disposition to make of the case. The disposition is roughly equivalent to the sentence in a criminal proceeding.

In making the disposition, the judge relies heavily on the expertise of probation officers who work with the court. Ideally, these professionals work to establish as complete an understanding of the juvenile as possible. They might do this by interviewing the youth and the responsible adults in his or her life, examining school and other relevant records, and having psychologists and other trained professionals perform diagnostic examinations and tests. Probation officers also often work closely with social workers to determine the availability of programs to help the youth. The judge can order whatever tests or evaluation procedures that he or she thinks will be helpful.

Probation officers then recommend a disposition plan to the judge at a disposition hearing. The juvenile, his or her lawyer, the parents, the victim of the crime, and others may also make recommendations.

Probation

Sixty percent of adjudicated delinquents receive some form of probation as their disposition. Probation can take many forms. Probation means that the youth is under the control of the court. In most cases, the youth is ordered to agree to certain conditions—perhaps to undergo drug counseling, or make financial restitution to the victim of their crime. A judge can set probation for a specific amount of time or leave it open-ended. Probation officers are responsible for monitoring the juvenile's progress, and the court holds regular review hearings to hear reports on the youth. When the judge

Probation officers also often work closely with social workers to determine the availability of programs to help the youth.

feels that the youth has fulfilled the conditions of probation, he or she ends the case.

Commitment

Thirty percent of adjudicated delinquents receive some form of residential commitment as part of their disposition. This represents a substantial increase—almost 40 percent—since the mid-1980s.

Residential commitment means that the youth is ordered to live in a facility, usually for a specific amount of time. Such facilities can range from group or family-like homes to prison-like secure juvenile facilities and may be either privately- or government-run. They are supposed to provide the youth with some kind of access to education or vocational training. Juveniles cannot be incarcerated with adults in adult prisons, however.

In some cases and jurisdictions, the judge decides to what specific institution the youth will be committed. In other cases and places, the judge places the juvenile in the jurisdiction of the state department of juvenile corrections, which then determines in what facility the youth will be placed and when the juvenile will be released.

Parole

Parole is a period of follow-up for a juvenile after he or she has been released from an institution. Upon release the judge or an officer for the state department of juvenile corrections sets conditions for parole. These conditions are often similar to those that are set for probation; the youth's compliance is monitored through meetings with parole officers and review hearings. If a juvenile violates parole by failing to comply with any of the conditions, he or she can be returned to commitment.

Summation

So is the new juvenile justice system, with its greater emphasis on punishment, working better than the old system? Is family court a kinder, wiser parent today?

As always with the justice system, it's hard to say. Some things can be said with certainty: More juveniles are being arrested than at any other time in the last three decades, for more violent crimes. In the last ten years alone, the juvenile arrest rate has risen by more than 20 percent. In 1997, the arrest rate for youths between ten and seventeen topped 9 percent, the highest in two decades. That year, law enforcement agencies made almost 3 million arrests of youths under the age of 18. The delinquency court caseload is more than four times what it was in 1960. More youths than ever before are tried as adults in criminal court. On any given day in this country, more than 100,000 youths are in some form of residential commitment.

So is youth crime truly an epidemic, as so many people have loudly proclaimed? Maybe. Scientists, doctors, and health professionals are usually the ones to be consulted about epidemics, and by the mid-1990s the National Academy of Sciences had little doubt about the underlying causes of the crime contagion: "Data from the Centers for Disease Control indicate that personal and neighborhood income are the strongest predictors of violent crime."

In other words, poverty is the single largest factor in juvenile crime. For children, there is an undeniable link between poverty, abuse, and crime. According to the Children's Defense Fund (CDF), the rate of abuse and neglect of children in families with an income near or below poverty level is seven times greater than for families with higher incomes. The CDF found that "being

For children, there is an undeniable link between poverty, abuse, and crime.

abused and neglected as a child increased the likelihood of arrest as a juvenile by 55 percent" and the likelihood of arrest for a violent crime by 38 percent.

Perhaps then it is no accident that a couple of other statistics indicate an increase in certain important categories almost equal to or greater than the rise in juvenile crime. Since 1980, more than 3 million children have been the subject of reports of abuse or neglect—an increase of about 161 percent. During that same time, the number of children living in poverty in the United States increased almost 30 percent. Today, one-fifth of all children in the richest and most powerful nation in the world live below the poverty level. That is a problem that neither treatment nor rehabilitation is likely to fix, which is something else about family court that you probably need to know.

Glossary

adjudication A judge's decision.

appeal To ask a higher court to review a lower court's decision.

capital punishment The use of execution as a legal sentence for a crime.

commitment In criminal and juvenile law, to deprive an individual of his or her physical freedom.

delinquent A legal term for juveniles who have been adjudicated as breaking the law.

dependency The portion of family court that deals with juveniles who have been neglected or abused.

disposition A judge's determination of how a youth who has been adjudicated delinquent should be handled.

diversion The process of removing a juvenile's case from the juvenile justice system for treatment elsewhere.

family preservation A legally mandated policy of dependency court that prevents the removal of children from their family unless absolutely necessary for their own safety and well-being.

family reunification A legally mandated policy of dependency court that requires that if children are removed from their home, they be placed with another family member before strangers.

hearing A type of legal proceeding, less formal than a trial. Family court proceedings are hearings rather than trials.

incarceration To be held in jail or prison.

in re Latin term used in the law meaning "in the matter of."

intake The process by which juveniles enter the family court system.

jurisdiction The legal authority of a court.

juvenile A youth who has not come of legal age.

parens patriae Latin phrase that roughly means "the parent is the state;" it is used to designate legal doctrine that is the basis for much juvenile law.

parole Disposition in a delinquency case that allows the court to monitor and treat a delinquent after he or she is released from commitment.

permanency planning A legally mandated policy of dependency court that requires the court to find a permanent solution to a dependent juvenile's problems as soon as possible.

petition A legal document requesting that a court perform a specific action.

probation A disposition in a delinquency case that requires a juvenile to meet certain conditions while being monitored by the court.

social worker An individual trained in the investigation, treatment, and material aid of the economically underprivileged and socially maladjusted.

station adjustment Diversion of juvenile offender given by police before the case enters the court system.

For Further Reading

Ayers, William. *A Kind and Just Parent: The Children of Juvenile Court.* Boston: Beacon, 1997.

Feld, Barry C. *Bad Kids: Race and the Transformation of Juvenile Court.* New York: Oxford, 1999.

Forer, Lois. *Unequal Protection: Women, Children, and the Elderly in Court.* New York: Norton, 1991.

Hawes, Joseph M. *The Children's Rights Movement in the United States: A History of Advocacy and Protection.* Boston: Twayne, 1991.

Hubner, John, and Jill Wolfson. *Somebody Else's Children: The Courts, the Kids, and the Struggle to Save America's Troubled Children.* New York: Three Rivers, 1996.

Humes, Edward. *No Matter How Loud I Shout: A Year in the Life of Juvenile Court.* New York: Touchstone, 1996.

U.S. Department of Health and Human Services. *Trends in the Well-Being of America's Children and Youth 1998.* Washington: U.S. Government Printing Office, 1999.

Vito, Gennaro F., Richard Tewksbury, and Deborah G. Wilson. *The Juvenile Justice System: Concepts and Issues.* Prospect Heights, IL: Waveland Press, 1999.

Where to
Go for Help

Center on Juvenile and Criminal Justice
2208 Martin Luther King Jr. Avenue, SE
Washington, DC 20020
(202) 678-9282
e-mail: cjcj@cjcj.org

Children's Defense Fund
25 E Street NW
Washington, DC 20001
(202) 628-8787
e-mail: cdfinfo@childrensdefense.org (or go to their
Web site for regional offices: http://www.childrensde-
fense.org/contacts.html)

Children's Rights Council
Suite 401, 300 I Street NE
Washington, DC 20002
(202) 547-6227

Juvenile Justice Center
American Bar Association
740 Fifteenth Street, NW, 10th Floor
Washington, DC 20005
(202) 662-1506
http://www.abanet.org

National Center on Institutes and Alternatives
Web site: http://www.ncianet.org

National Consortium on Alternatives for Youth at Risk
5250 Seventeenth Street, Suite 107
Sarasota, Florida 34235-8247
(941) 378-4793
(800) 245-7133
Web site: http://www.ncayar
e-mail: ncayar@worldnet.att.net

United States Department of Justice
Office of Juvenile Justice and Delinquency Prevention
Washington, DC 20531
Web site: http://www.ojjdp.ncjrs.org
see also United States Department of Justice Kids' Page
Web site: http://www.usdoj.gov.kids.page

Index

A
Addams, Jane, 18, 19, 20–21, 24, 32
adjudication, 33, 51–52
abuse, 22

B
bail, 41

C
capital punishment, 15–16, 23
Children's Defense Fund (CDF), 56
child welfare courts, 29, 31, 32, 35
commitment, 54–55
constitutional protections, 40, 41
criminal court, 12, 26, 30, 31, 32, 34, 39, 40, 41, 42, 50–51, 52, 56
criminal justice system, 13–14, 23, 51–52
custody, 29, 34, 39, 42

D
death penalty, 16, 22
delinquency, 28, 29, 30, 34, 36, 39, 40, 42, 43, 47, 51, 52
delinquency court, 29, 44, 46, 56
delinquency hearing, 31, 32, 36, 41, 51
delinquents, 26, 27, 33, 34, 35, 49, 53, 54
dependency, 28, 29, 44
dependency court, 29, 34, 35, 42–45, 49

detention, 49–50
disposition, 33, 34, 35, 44, 53–54

E
Eighth Amendment, 16, 41

F
family court, 12, 13, 17, 18, 24, 26, 27, 28, 29, 30, 31, 32, 39, 40, 43, 46, 49, 55
family preservation, 44
family reunification, 45
First Great Wave of Immigration, 19
foster home, 43, 45

G
group homes, 34
guns, in schools, 7, 9, 11

H
hearing, 30, 32, 33, 37, 39, 50, 54, 55
homicide rate, 9, 11
Hull House, 18

I
immigrants, 19–21
incarceration, 22
intake, 47, 49
intake officers, 49
In re Gault, 36, 40
In re Winship, 40, 51

J

jurisdiction, 12, 27, 28, 29, 30, 32, 35, 46, 50, 51, 55

juvenile homes, 33

Juvenile Justice and Delinquency Prevention Act (JJDPA), 52

juvenile court (juvenile justice system), 12, 24, 27, 28, 29, 35, 42, 55

L

legal rights, 27, 31, 35

legal system, 12, 15, 21, 22, 24, 28

N

Nineteenth Amendment, 17

Nobel Peace Prize, 18

P

parens patriae, 26–27, 43

parole, 55

petition, 32, 33, 36, 40, 41, 49

poverty, 12, 14, 20, 22, 24, 25, 43, 57

probation, 53–54, 55

probation officers, 27, 33, 34, 36, 47, 49, 53

Progressives, 24–25

punishment, 8, 17, 21–23, 31, 34, 40, 42, 55

R

rehabilitation, 17, 21–23, 24, 26, 31, 34, 35, 40, 42

rights, 39, 40

S

settlement houses, 18–19

shelters, 34, 45

Sixth Amendment, 41

social environment, 12, 24, 25

social welfare agency, 13, 26, 39

social workers, 18, 27, 33, 34, 43, 44, 49

station adjustment, 47

status offenders, 47–49, 52, 53

T

Thirteenth Amendment, 16

U

U.S. Centers for Disease Control, 11, 56

U.S. Constitution, 16, 25, 39, 41

U.S. Department of Justice, 52

U.S. Supreme Court, 15–16, 36, 39, 40, 51

V

violent crime, 10, 11, 24, 53, 56

vocational schools, 33

About the Author

Anne Bianchi is a Legal Aid attorney in New York state who often represents juveniles. She is a graduate of Antioch Law School in Washington, DC.

Photo Credits

Cover and inside photos by Ira Fox. Pp. 17 & 19 © CORBIS.

Design and Layout: Annie O'Donnell